Crystal Healing

(The Definitive Guide)

Therapy for Healing, Increasing Energy, Strengthening Spirituality, Improving Health and Attracting Wealth

Table of Contents

Introduction

Chapter 1: About Crystal Healing and Therapy

Chapter 2: How Crystal Therapy works

Chapter 3: A Brief Overview of Types of Crystals

Chapter 4: The Step by Step uses for Crystals

Chapter 5: Méditation Techniques for Crystals

Chapter 6: Caring for Crystals

Chapter 7: Crystals for Healing and Recovery

Chapter 8: Crystals for Strengthening Spirituality

Chapter 9: Crystals for Improving Physical Health

Chapter 10: Crystals for Energy & Clarity

Chapter 11: Crystals for Wealth and Abundance

Chapter 12: Crystals for Happiness and Fulfillment

Chapter 13: Further Online Resources and Tools

Conclusion

Introduction

Welcome. Firstly I would like to thank you for purchasing this Critically Acclaimed Best Selling book "Crystal Healing". This book contains a wealth of information for both the Crystal Healing Beginner, and the Crystal Healing Expert.

Have you been looking for a reliable and proven alternative medicine for healing? One that doesn't require you to be taking extreme doses of medications? Would you rather use a healing method that requires no drugs or lab engineered chemicals? Are you sick of always visiting the doctor, and getting minimal results?

There is a healing process that demands neither drugs nor syringes; all you need is a couple of well-chosen crystals, determination, and knowledge. I know it sounds too good to be true, especially if it's your first time encountering the method, but trust me, modern crystal healing practices are offered in both professional clinics and wellness spas throughout the world.

One of the best things about crystal healing is its versatility. The practice acts both as a preventive measure and also can heal you from illnesses in a reactive manner too. Remember those times when you take pain relievers? Usually after popping these pills, you will feel relieved, but often the headache will return because you did not attend to the real cause. Crystal healing is better option in these instances, because it heals you holistically, addressing the problem at the cause level, when then relieves the symptoms.

Some are usually afraid to try a new healing process, it's not difficult at all, and contrary to popular belief, you do not need to be psychic (or have any other special ability) to use crystals. With this book beside you, you will be guided accordingly. You will learn everything from the "rationale" behind crystal healing, proper ways of taking care of your crystals, how will you choose them, and what crystals will you need for a certain purposes.

Aside from health, crystals are also great for other aspects of your life, such as happiness, fulfillment, career, and wealth. It really is amazing the power that Crystals hold. They are by far the most underrated health and life wellness tool of the 21st century. All of these uses, will also be discussed in this book in great detail.

So, with no further delay, lets get into things !

Chapter 1: About Crystal Healing and Therapy

In this section, we will learn three key things: what crystals are, a little bit of its history from different countries and faiths, and the benefits that you can obtain from using crystals in healing.

What are Crystals?

Crystals are homogeneous substances (often in solid form) that are formed over long periods of time, from different geological processes: some crystals are created from magma, others from ice, and others from mollusks. Our ancestors, however, had their first fill of crystals while they were exploring Mother Nature. Usually, most crystals can be found from the bedrock.

Like any other matter, Crystals are made up of atoms. But unlike other matter, the atoms of crystals are strategically arranged. This arrangement is the key to their effectiveness. We will discuss more about this later in the next chapter.

Crystals are extremely strong and hardy. They are very resistant to wear and tear that people often use them as jewellery or body ornaments. Quite often, they even became a part of our interior home and office design.

History of Crystals in Different Countries and Faith

The truth is, people have been using crystals for more than 30,000 years. Even without the proper scientific knowledge, our ancestors have already acknowledged the power of crystals in healing and energizing.

Experts believe that the first usage of crystals originated from Atlantis, but since it is the land that never was, there were no decent records to prove it. What we have, instead are records from Egypt. Although historians bravely disagree on the notion that crystal energies were responsible for the erection of the Egyptian pyramids, they cannot argue on the fact that people in Egypt used crystal to formulate powerful healing potions. Greeks, also have a long history with crystals. In fact, the word crystal translates to the Greek word which means "ice".

In China and India, the most popular gemstone before was jade because of its terrific healing property. If you'll notice, Indians even have the famous Kapa Tree used in Hinduism-- it has 9 gems hanging from the branches.

Christianity also had its fair share of contribution to the fame of crystals. Representation of the tribes of Israel was made by assigning one crystal for each tribe. The gems used are the following: Lapiz lazuli, jasper, onyx, agate, amethyst, zircon, emerald, sapphire, turquoise, aquamarine, ruby, and topaz.

Benefits of Crystals in Healing

There are many benefits of crystal healing, the first of which is the fact that crystal therapy is a **non-invasive form of making the body feel better**. Unlike going to the hospital, it needs no syringes and it definitely won't require you to take in any form of chemical medications. Crystal healing can be achieved through the laying of stones, placing it under the pillow, including crystals in your bath water, and keeping the crystals close to your body. None of those methods hurts nor harms you.

Second is, crystal healing **has many facets**. It can be used for bodily aches, it can clear your mind, make you feel at ease, drive away negative energy, and even protect you from others' wrath. People even use crystals to attract money or career improvement.

Another benefit to crystal healing is its **inexpensiveness.** Crystals are best used for health promotion and disease prevention. If you incorporate crystal healing in your life, you will avoid visiting the hospital in the long run. You won't need to purchase medications, and you won't need t undergo surgeries. All you need to do is to choose the correct crystals for you.

And lastly, crystal healing is very much **personalized**. You can ask or assess yourself what the problem is, and you can find the corresponding crystal to heal it. You can also choose from various methods-- it does not always have to be laying of stones. That way, you will be more comfortable, and in comfort, you reduce stress.

Chapter 2: How Crystal Therapy works

Our ancestors have long since acknowledged the benefits of crystal healing, but they were not able to provide us with scientific proofs. In fact, what they had were mere attachments to nature and magic. But notice the spas around you... most of them will also offer services like crystal therapy or gemstone healing. If the rationale behind this non-invasive form of healing is mere magic, then why are spas worldwide offering it to the general clientele?

Perhaps, even you. You have doubts regarding how a piece of stone can help you feel better. You might also be wondering why scientists do not pour enough effort into crystal healing research. The answer to that question is simple: crystals are unlike medications. When a medication is not well-tested, it can harm people because they are being ingested, injected, or applied over the skin. Scientists really have to make sure that they are safe through experiments and research studies. Crystals, on the other hand, have little risk-- no need to put too much effort because they are virtually harmless.

Don't worry though; crystal healing is still backed with scientific facts.

What is Dominant Oscillatory Rate?

Dominant Oscillatory Rate (DOR) is how we vibrate. According to scientists, everything in the universe, down to the smallest unit, is a vibration. That means, we, humans are vibrating. Each and every one of our cells operates in different vibrational frequencies, but they operate in harmony. In that harmony, we are healthy.

When we are suffering from an illness or even psychological stress, the harmony is being disrupted. Our DOR becomes chaotic. It is only when our vibrational frequency is stable can the healing process begin.

Crystals are Geometrically Perfect

The good news is, getting the harmony back is not impossible. In fact, experts tell us that our bodies are capable of restoring it, what we need is a little push or a little help. Where do we get that help? Where else? In crystal therapy!

Now, here's where the scientific explanation takes place. Crystals, like us, are also made of vibrations. The only difference is this: they are perfect, at least, geometrically speaking.

The atoms of crystals are arranged in a definite pattern, and this pattern makes them very stable, including the vibrational frequency that they release. Unlike humans, the DOR of crystals cannot be changed or damaged, no matter what the circumstances are. In fact, this particular property is what makes crystals truly unique among all other matters.

If we keep them close to our body, then it will help our body attain the harmonious DOR that we desire for. Once the steady frequency is back, recovery from an illness will commence.

Knowing the scientific basis of crystal healing is very important because it will keep your mind at ease. You will know that what you are doing is not a waste of time. In some cases, people try to heal using crystals but they find it ineffective because they do not believe in its power.

Chapter 3: A Brief Overview of Types of Crystals

Crystals can be classified according to their shape and purpose. These two classifications are both important because they play a part in comfort and effectiveness.

According to Shapes

You might be wondering: why are shapes important if the geometrical structure of crystals is already perfect? It's quite simple: crystal therapy requires you to have the crystals close to your body. You have to know what crystals are best for laying of the stones, what are best to be used as jewellery, and what are best used as decorative ornaments. You can determine it by learning about their shapes or forms.

Single Terminated Wands: These are elongated crystals. One end is unformed, while the other end is pointed. Most of the time, people use this as an interior ornament, bu they can also be placed beside the body while meditating.

Chunks: If you want crystals that can be carried in your pocket, you may as well look for chunks. They have no definite shapes, their sizes also vary, and they have rough exteriors.

Clusters: Clusters are easy to spot because they look like a bunch of crystals attached together. This is an ordinary form because crystals really come in pairs. Crystal enthusiasts often choose clusters when they want to improve the atmosphere in their home or office.

Cut: Do you remember going inside a crystal shop and seeing that one crystal with a perfect shape, like a pyramid? Well, that's a cut crystal. Cuts are processed: they are polished and shaped so that they will look good.

Tumblestones: Are also polished stones, but they are smaller. They are perfect for the laying of stones, but they can also be carried in your pocket. They come in different shapes and sizes.

According to Purpose

You also have to choose crystals according to their purpose. One crystal can have two or more purposes so don't worry about running out of options. Understanding the information below will help you select the best crystal for your current situation.

Energizing: As the name suggests, energizing crystals are capable of lending you strength on times when you feel weak. Or perhaps, you are not feeling weak, but you are undergoing a particularly hard challenge and you feel like you could use more energy. These crystals have very strong DOR that's why they are energized.

Just quick reminders though, do not use them often and do not keep these crystals near you during bedtime because they may disrupt your sleep. If you need to use them frequently, then be sure to wrap them in a piece of cloth first.

Chakra balancing: There are 7 chakra points in the body, and when one or two of them is blocked or unbalanced, we may experience physiological and psychological stress. Chakra balancing crystals aim to restore the unbalanced or blocked wheels of energy that we have.

Grounding: Don't mistake this as the crystal that will hold you down. People often think that grounding crystals prevent them from achieving their dreams, that's not true.

Grounding crystals are used to make sure that you do not become too caught up in your
success. Successful people keep this crystal close to them to make sure that they do not forget their roots.

Manifesting: If you are suffering from negativities, manifesting crystals are perfect for you. They open your mind into many opportunities and they encourage you to take risks.

Love: Problems with romance? Then select a love crystal that can attract affection. More than that, they also encourage you to be more compassionate to yourself and others.

Record Keeping: Students and career people love record keeping crystals because they are capable of improving your memory. Crystal users say that when they have record keeping crystals, memorization becomes easier.

Meditation: If you want to connect more with yourself, try meditating. If you want your meditation to be more effective, then have some meditation crystals near you while doing it.

Shielding: Are you worried that someone will hurt you? Do you want to prevent the negative vibration from getting near you? If these are your desires, then purchase a shielding crystal. They are capable of protecting you from bad vibes.

Chapter 4: The Step by Step uses for Crystals

In this chapter, you will know how to heal yourself using crystals. Ultimately, there are just three steps, after you have done these three steps, you can proceed on the laying of the stones, or if you are not comfortable in that method, you can choose from other alternatives.

Step #1 - Choosing the correct crystal

Choosing the crystals are very important because you have to feel at ease with them. Like a friend, you should also trust them. If you do not believe in your crystals, then it surely won't help you heal.

Here are the steps on how to choose crystals:

Blind method: blind method seems weird for some people, but a lot see its simplicity and thus, opt to choose their crystals using this way. While in the store, close your eyes and do deep breathings. Take as many deep breaths as you like until you feel your whole body relax. Once relaxed, imagine yourself picking a stone. Remember that while you do this, your eyes are closed. Carefully trudge to the direction you see in your mind and pick the crystal.

It may feel weird, but don't worry. Crystal shops accommodate this method frequently.

Precise method: The precise method is simpler and if you feel weird about the blind method, then you can choose this one. What you need to do is enter the shop and "feel" all the crystals. That means you look at each one of them and you must touch them too. After you have felt everything, you can decide. What crystal makes you feel most comfortable? What is your favorite? Choose the crystal that stands out for you.

Internet shopping: Internet shopping is tricky because you cannot "feel" the crystals. You can rectify the situation by talking to an expert. Online crystal shops often have experts willing to assist you. If there is no one, then do the blind method- screen style.

Step #2 -Cleansing

The next step is to cleanse your crystal. You always have to clean your crystals after purchasing it so as to make sure that there are no lingering negative energies. You also have to clean your crystals every once in a while, especially if it no longer feels good.

There are different ways to cleanse the stones, you can use one method each time you cleanse or you can also choose different methods with each session.

Smudging: To do smudging, you have to light up some of the incense and let the smoke clean the crystals. Smudging will only take 30 minutes to complete.

Moonlight: Moonlight also has the power to get rid of the negative energies. Leave your crystals in a place where the moon can shine on it. Leave it overnight (the duration is up to you), but be sure to take it back before the sun rises because sunlight can discolor the crystals.

Use of herbs: Take a bowl and fill it with assortment of herbs, bury your crystals in the herbs and leave it for days or even weeks. After this, throw the herbs away because they are tainted with negative energies.

Burying: If you feel particularly bad about your crystals and you believe it needs a deep cleansing, bury it in the soil for a few days.

The pointed part of the stones should be directed downwards. Place a marker on the spot so that you won't get confused when it's time to dig them out.

Visualization: Hold the crystal in front of you and imagine a light stream pass through it. As the light passes through, visualize the negative energies being thrown away from the crystal.

Running water: Hold your crystal under the faucet and make sure that the pointed part is directed downwards. Let the running water "wash" the crystal. It may take as short as 5 minutes to complete, depending on how tainted your crystals are.

Step #3 -Programming

After cleansing your crystal, the next step is to program it. Programming means you will dedicate the crystal to your desires. For example, you purchased the crystal because you wanted to have a more fulfilling relationship with your partner. Program the crystal by meditating.

Find a serene place in your house and relax. Hold your crystal close to you and imagine your desires and visualize them coming true. Dream of all the things that will happen once you have a healthy, loving relationship with your partner. Think deeply about it and enforce your thoughts on the stone.

Do this several times until you feel that your stone already shares the same desires as you.

Step #4 - Laying of the Stones and the 7 Chakra Points

Laying of the stones is typically done with a psychic, but it helps a lot if you know what to expect. You will be asked to lie on your back on the floor or mattress. The psychic will then lay the crystals on different chakra point of you body. He or she will touch each of the crystals and will imagine a light passing through it-- taking away all the illnesses or discomfort that you feel. After that, the psychic will flick a finger to make sure that the negative energies are released before moving on to the next stone.

To have a clear picture of where the psychic will be placing the stones, let us discuss the different chakra points. Chakras are wheels of energies that travel all around the body through channels or points. When these points are troubled (either imbalanced or blocked), illnesses can happen.

Crown: This chakra point regulates your brain. If you often experience headaches, confusion, incoordination, or other central nervous system problems, then perhaps you are having trouble with the crown chakra. It can be found at the top of the head.

Third Eye: Are you having problems with your eyes, ears, nose or bones? Then perhaps your Third Eye chakra is blocked or imbalanced. This chakra point found between the eyes is also responsible for your intelligence and intuition.

Throat: Throat chakra can be found at the "V" of your neck. Crystal healing experts say that this is the one responsible for self expression. Respiratory health is also associated with this point.

Heart: If you lack compassion and affection, perhaps your heart chakra is blocked or imbalanced. This chakra point is also related to heart problems and other circulatory system illnesses.

Solar Plexus: The chakra for the digestive system, solar plexus chakra point is also responsible for your passions. When we say passion, it's everything from eagerness, anger, and ego. Find this chakra point between your ribs and belly button.

Sacral: Slightly lower than your navel, this chakra point is responsible for a person's reproductive organs issues. If you are having fertility problems, you must consider having your sacral chakra cleared.

Root: Root chakra is your grounding chakra-- it keeps you "rooted". This can be found at base of the spine. If you feel insecure, and frequently you feel as if everything will fall apart, concentrate on this point. Weight problems are also associated with this chakra.

Chapter 5: Méditation Techniques for Crystals

Meditation is done to connect with yourself. It can relieve you off the stress, and it can make you reflect on what's happening in your life. If you are wondering how to incorporate crystals in your meditation, then follow these simple meditation techniques for crystals.

Visualization

Often, in many visualization techniques, practitioners imagine a safe place, a comfort zone, where they can feel free to tackle on an energy source. You should use a quartz crystal, as it will be easier to actually connect with its power, because it's transparent. But feel free to use another stone, because, with a little imagination you can make any stone your comfort zone.

The first thing you need to do is learn your crystal. The outside and the inside, including its purpose and the type of energy it radiates. See if it has any cracks, gaps, characteristic patterns and other features. If you take a piece of rhyolite crystal, even as a none transparent stone, you can still make it your home for the meditation. It has many see-through "windows" (quartz loops that create tiny tunnels) which will spark your imagination.

So let's say you chose a rhyolite for your visualization. Rhyolites are usually green, with yellow, white, red or orange irregular shapes. Take it in your hand or place it in front of you. Close your eyes and take a few deep breaths. As you breathe in, imagine the stone spreading its rays towards you. Imagine the energy touching you. Imagine it going through you and surrounding you. All of its colors are hugging you and making your skin tone the same pattern as your stone. Now you and your stone have become the same being. There is no you and it anymore, you are one.

Now imagine your stone growing in front of you or in your hands. With each breath the stone is bigger. When it becomes big enough, you can go inside, sit quietly and watch the world from its colorful windows. Let your imagination run free and make a comfortable space for you to sit inside your stone. You don't really know what's inside, so there can be your favorite chair, a nice comfy sofa or a blossoming meadow. Pick whatever feels right. Sit there silently and let the images present themselves. The crystal will help you to dig deep in your heart and find the answer you are looking for.

Or not.

Not everything is about answers. Sometimes you just need a safe haven where you can rest and not think about anything. Or you can take a journey while you are in this state of being in the stone you are holding. You can go to the past or the future. You can rehearse for an interview, meet a special someone or see yourself 10 years from now. You can go back in time and see what you did wrong, correct your mistake or apologize to someone you've wronged. It's totally up to you how you want to use the energy from the stone, which is a powerful and insightful source.

Third Eye Beaming

The third eye is the chakra that knows everything. It knows our true thoughts, their root and gives birth to our intuition. When this energy vortex is blocked or tainted, we think in terms of greed, power plays and manipulation. We paint a picture of a reality that's not real, but fits our agenda nicely. If you try to receive energy through this chakra and you can't, or the source is blurred or weak, it means that the third eye is not working properly. You need to cleanse this chakra and spin it, to make it guide you on the right path again. We will talk about crystals for this chakra later, for now let's learn how to clean this compass.

You should lay on a bed because the crystal has to be placed between your eyebrows. You can massage this spot with your index finger in upward motions, as if you are opening an eyelid. Once the crystal is in its place, you can relax and start breathing. Imagine all your bad thoughts as little dark specks. Don't try to define them, because if your third eye is blocked you may not even acknowledge them all. Your third eye knows what they are and it will collect them without you picking favorites. For now, just listen to your breathing and try to imagine the dark specks in your head. They are trying to stay stuck to your brain, but the crystal between your brows has opened the vacuum and they are forced out. With each breath in, they gather in a tiny stream and with each breath out, the stream is rushing out of your third eye. Nothing can stop this process now, because your third eye is wide open. Let all the specks get out, and once the last one is out, you can take a few deep breaths to fill the head with new, fresh oxygen.

Now, the time has come to recharge your brain with new, positive, constructive and loving thoughts. Don't try to name them either. Let the crystal filter the good vibrations. All you need to do is imagine a fresh stream pouring into your head, through the third eye. The stream is clean and blue like a mountain waterfall. Deep and refreshing. You can feel every inch of your head being filled with this new, fresh energy. Once you feel restored and revitalized, you can imagine the third eye closing up until it becomes the size of an iris. This little dot on your forehead is now pulsating with light and filtering all of your future thoughts.

Breathing Meditation

Breathing exercises are the basis of meditation. By listening to your breath you will learn to focus your attention inwards, instead of outwards. If you are a beginner, you might lose focus even in these first steps, so that's why you should use a mantra typically applied in breathing exercises to help you concentrate. The words "so" and "hum" (or ham) come from the Sanskrit word Soham, which means I Am He/It/That. According to the story, when a baby is born, it cries Koham, which means: Who Am I? To which the universe replies: Soham, trying to let the newborn realize that it is a part of the universe, or ultimately – the universe itself.

Place your crystal where you can see it and gaze in it. Phase out everything else in the room and just look at the crystal. With each breath, mentally say So. With every exhale, say Hum. Focus your eyes on the crystal and your mind on those two words. You can do this exercise anywhere from 5 to 20 minutes, or longer if you don't get bored. Remember to say these words in your mind. This is important if you are a beginner, because your mind will wander a lot and you might have troubles concentrating. But if you focus on saying the words in your mind, your mind won't have the time to think about anything else. It's not possible to think about two things at once.

Subtle Energy Techniques

We sense energy all around us all the time, because we are all made entirely of energy. On a molecular level, every bodily organ, breath we take and surface we touch is pure energy. It's just that, everybody feels those energies differently. Some people sense those energies through their hands, some through the change of emotions or feelings about a subject, other people don't feel them at all. The chakras on the human body are a buildup energy field you can sense very easily. It will be better to learn how your own energy works, but another person can also be a great test energy field. The basic 7 chakras are aligned along the spine of the human body, staring from the tailbone and ending at the top of the head.

Rub your hands together before you start, to spark up your own energy. Release all the tension you are holding and order all your senses to be alert and open up. Start with the base chakra, the one on your tailbone. Place your hand over your pubic area, or just under it, between your legs. Don't touch, just feel. Move your hand slowly up and stop at every chakra. See if you feel anything different. You may feel dizzy or nauseous. You may suddenly feel pain somewhere in the body. Your nose might start dripping or your ears might be buzzing. You might start feeling sad, happy or an image might reveal itself. You might feel your hands warming up or cooling down. Every new sensation you feel will be an indication that you are sensing the energy from your chakras. You can also do this exercise with a pendulum, which will also tell you in which direction the chakras are spinning.

Once you learn to feel your energy vortexes, you can easily clean them and set them spinning in the right direction. Usually, men's chakras spin clockwise, while women's counterclockwise that way they complement each other, as yin and yang. This is not a rule, however and yours might spin differently. You should visit an energy healer to tell you how exactly to work with your chakras. Otherwise, you might spin them in the wrong direction. If you are not sure about their direction, you can still open them and heal them with a crystal wand. A wand it is not just a magical tool, it is also a healing tool. Start by pointing it down, to the earth. Imagine a beam of energy growing up from the earth and going into your wand. Move your wand over each chakra and hold it still for a couple of seconds. Let the earth energy fill each chakra and once you feel the vortex is full, move on to the next one. When you get to the crown chakra and cleanse it, raise your hand up and let the energy from the earth, go through your chakras, through your entire body and send it up to the universe.

Chapter 6: Caring for Crystals

How to care for crystals

Taking care of your crystals is the same thing as caring for a pet or a plant. If you believe setting up an altar just for your stones is a little medieval scene for your home, it doesn't give you the right to toss them aside and never look at them again. Consider them as beings that exude energy and they shouldn't be kept in the dark.

Some people though, choose to keep their stones in a pouch or in a drawer. This is a great home for your crystals if many people go into the room where you keep them. Crystals will not choose whom they share, absorb or transform energy, so you should avoid letting other people touch them, or hold them for too long. They will respond to every vibration in the room, regardless if it's yours or someone else's. You can also keep them in a jewelry box, but make sure they are wrapped in a gentle cloth. Quartz crystals, amethyst, tourmaline and few other stones are fragile and they may chip off pieces if they dropped on a hard surface.

Crystals love being put up on a pedestal. You don't need to buy special stands or make them platforms, they just like to stand alone in a place that will be known as theirs. You can arrange them around a long burning candle, display them on your night table or dedicate a place in your home, where they can be out of the sight of many people.

If you choose to keep them out of a box, you will need to clean them more often. Again, it all depends on how much outside stimuli they get throughout the day. If you exude negative feelings and emotions, or use them in body healings, your crystals need to be recharged before and after every session.

If your stones lose their gleam, start to crack on their own or you feel repelled when you hold them, it means that they have built up energy debris from their surroundings. Cleansing them is now necessary.

Should you keep crystals for the rest of your life?

There is no rule saying that you must keep your crystal to yourself your entire life. Sometimes you may unconsciously pick a crystal that will help you get rid of some emotional baggage or get you through a tough period. You may find out that you don't really like the crystal after it helps you through a certain change. This is not bad and you are not a bad person. It is said that crystals choose you long before you choose, or even set your eyes on them, so use their guidance.

Loosing or breaking stones is not a tragedy or a bad omen either. This is also the crystal's way of telling you that you don't need it anymore. Still, if you get too attached to your crystals, you'll feel like losing a dear friend. It will be best to give them away to someone, add them to your fish bowl or bury them in your garden. When you feel you have lost the special bond with a stone, show it to other people. If you see a spark in their eyes, it means the crystal has found its new owner.

Chapter 7: Crystals for Healing and Recovery

Amber

This is a widely used stone, dating back 8000 years before our century. Amber is not an actual stone or crystal. It's a fossilized resin, sometimes containing seeds, insects and parts of the plant that got stuck to the sticky tree balm thousands of years ago. Kept around your aura, it will improve your blood circulation, boost the immune system, relieve joint and muscle pains and clean your body from toxins. Many traditions around the world use this powerful healer to guard children's health and psychic attacks. Teething pains become bearable when a necklace is worn made of amber beads. To feel its healing effects faster, make sure the resin is touching your skin, like in a form of earrings, necklace or a ring.

Hematite

This ancient stone has always been used for healing. In many cultures people believe that placed over the affected area, this stone will soak up the illness or pain. It's made of iron and oxygen, which will help in all blood related complaints, like anemia, clotting, menstruation, toxicity and etc. You can use it to relieve pains in broken bones and fractures. It is a grounding stone that works best on the root chakra, where it will help your body generate new energy to work with. Some people are sensitive to its power, so try to test it first before you use it in healings directly on the skin.

Ametrine

This crystal is part amethyst, part citrine. A wonderful combination for soothing discomfort of long-term diseases, like HIV and cancer. It will help you to balance your emotions and quiet the thoughts full of anger, grief and fear. It is a stone for clearing the energy in your room, by standing proud on your nightstand. You can also use it in third eye meditations.

Chapter 8: Crystals for Strengthening Spirituality

Amethyst

This stone is excellent for beginners. Its energy is radiated instantly and you will feel a light glow surrounding your entire body once you hold it. It's actually many people's first choice in crystals, because it emits loving rays received from afar. The deep purple amethyst pieces (as well as chevron amethyst) will raise your awareness and connect you to a higher realm. You can use it in prayers and meditations. Its accepting energy will make you more humble and kind. You can develop your intuition with this crystal and clear your mind from negative thinking patterns. Amethyst will protect you from energy vampires, by either making them more submissive around you, or avoiding your protective glow altogether.

Anhydrite or Angelite

Both of these stones come from the same mineral, and they are used for the same purpose – spiritual growth. Just as the name indicates, Angelite will connect you to beings from higher realms. It will ease your connection to god, the universe, the angels or any other transcendent presence you believe in. It is used for opening the throat, third eye and crown chakra, and sends your thoughts and energy to your soul star chakra. It is an excellent crystal for deep meditation and receiving information from the akashic records. You can use it for meditation practices, or place it under your pillow at night.

Labradorite

This is a highly mystical stone and just by looking at its translucent texture, you will feel carried away to a higher state of consciousness. Illusions and lies are dispelled with this stone. You will have to be ready to see the true reality and true intentions when you use this stone. It is especially good for making a change. It will help your lock your aura from outward energies.

Fluorite

All forms of fluorite found in nature will help you develop your third eye chakra and open up your energetic body to the cosmic energy. It is an excellent crystal for beginners, because it helps you stay focused and grounded during meditation. You will understand your purpose in the world with regular use of this stone, and it will also assist you in voicing your thoughts and wishes when communicating with celestial energies. It is a great stone to assist you in turning your thoughts into actions and results.

Chapter 9: Crystals for Improving Physical Health

Red jasper

This is another stone used since ancient times. Warriors were carrying this stone with them to increase their endurance and physical stamina during their long battles. Held in a hand, it will create a positive atmosphere around the holder, after hospitalization, long term illnesses or injuries. Its red color is associated with blood and healthy muscle tissue, so have it with you after muscle ruptures, strains or during training. It can also help you in detoxifying processes and removing blockages in the bile duct and liver. It is a stone that works slowly on your energetic body, but the longer you have it with you, the stronger it becomes. It doesn't need frequent cleansing like other crystals. In ancient times, both future and new mothers were wearing this stone. It promotes fertility, healthy fetus growth and safe child birth. It can also amplify the fertility process, in both, men and women. Red jasper can also help in healing many ailments of reproductive system.

Bloodstone

This green stone with red spots will help your blood circulation. If you place several pieces around your home, it will also clean the energy and move it around. It's a great stone for placing in the room of sick people and gives strength when held in hand. Meditation with bloodstone absorbs the blocks from the chakras, as well as blocks preventing the internal organs from working properly.

Yellow Jasper

This stone also takes time to activate and attune with your energetic body. You can carry it with you in a pouch or pocket to pull strength from it. It is a great stone to have with you during a hangover and placed near or below the solar chakra, it will clean your lower organs from toxins, such as alcohol. It's a great anti-vomiting aid.

Chapter 10: Crystals for Energy & Clarity

Black Onyx

This black crystal will help you preserve your energy during times of stress and exhaustion. It will also transform all you negative energy into positive and help you protect it from energy drainers. All black stones, but especially onyx, give the wearer courage, decision making abilities and protect the body from physical harm. You can wear it in a form of an accessory.

Calcite

The orange calcite is a powerful energy amplifier. It works really fast and you can feel its effects after wearing it very shortly. You don't need to place it on a special chakra because this gem automatically finds the tension and stress you are hiding in the body and releases it. It is known as the crystal for the mind, because it can help you retain information and make you very analytical. It is a great stone to have nearby when studying or having disagreements. It is usually used in healing the first two chakras, where it will stimulate motivation, drive and healthy energy expenditure.

Apache Tears

This precious gem is great for people who are stuck in the same emotional and mental patterns. It will open your horizons and help you create a new attitude towards old problems. Even as a distinct form of obsidian, apache tears hold a lot of the properties of the obsidian crystal. They are grounding, balancing, and will help you get rid of the feelings magnified by an overactive root chakra, like greed, jealousy, resentment and rage.

Chapter 11: Crystals for Wealth and Abundance

Green Aventurine

Known as the "gambler's stone" green aventurine is carried for good luck and prosperity. Its green color resembles the many riches our mother earth provides in abundance. It is used for both healing and money rituals and meditations, and if you want to attract more money, keep it in your wallet, cash box or safe. Regular exposure to its energy will heighten your perception and sharpen your intelligence.

Tiger's Eye

This is a semi-precious gem used for refining personal energy. It will amplify your best characteristic to make you a leader and authority in a group. It works best with the solar plexus chakra, where it will connect your ideas and dreams from the upper chakras and draw them down to your lower chakras, where it gives you the will and drive to turn them into reality.

Pyrite

This gem is called "fool's gold" because it has been foolishly mistaken for gold in the past. Its masculine energy will help you tap into your own limitless potential. Just like tiger's eye, pyrite too will make you assertive in situations where you need to take on a leading role. It will help you balance the power between you and a manipulating or controlling employer. Tiredness, fatigue and intellectual blockages will be dispelled, while self-worth, confidence and enthusiasm will be heightened when you have this mineral in your workplace or office.

Lapis Lazuli

This is a stone mainly used for divination, but as a throat chakra opener, it will help you voice out your ideas and give you confidence in presenting them. It is a powerful aid for public speakers and people who need to sound convincing and wise.

Chapter 12: Crystals for Happiness and Fulfillment

Malachite

This is said to be one of the most important and powerful crystals. Beginners may have troubles working with this stone, because it amplifies, both negative and positive energy, so you need to be trained or at least, very careful when you use it. It will be best to have it near you when you meditate with another stone, as it will enhance the other stone's properties. Used alone, it can help you get rid of old emotional traumas you are carrying around. It will open your heart chakra and balance your emotions. Especially good for people who often let themselves fall in emotional extremes, whether that is rage and aggression, or shyness and humility.

Rhyolite

This stone is another great hearth chakra opener. It can help you understand karma, and the relationship between the past, present and future. You can work with this stone on healing old emotional wounds that rob you of happiness and fulfillment. It brings joy and acceptance of the way things are. It relieves depression and lethargy.

Quartz Crystals

These minerals are called "master healers" in the metaphysical world. They are extremely versatile, they can work with any chakra and help you heal yourself of any ailment. Rose quartz is commonly used for opening the heart chakra, from where you can find love for all beings. It is the easiest crystal to work with because you can easily connect with it, which will further unite (harmonize) you with the rest of the universe. Best given as a present to a loved one, a friend or a lover.

Chapter 13: Further Online Resources and Tools

Websites

Emily Gems

Emily Gems is an online store that sells crystals and gemstones. They also provide you with great information about chakra, Feng Sui, stone meanings and color interpretation. Each crystal is sold at different forms and prices so you will have a lot of choices.

https://crystal-cure.com/crystal-healing.html

Healing Crystals For You

This website is a one stop shop if you want to have a detailed descriptions and interpretation of the stones and crystals. You can even share your own story about crystal healing!

http://www.healing-crystals-for-you.com/

Books

The Crystal Bible: A Definitive Guide to Crystals

This book is completely illustrated and the information is detailed: from colors, shapes and application, both beginners and experts will love having this book around.

https://www.goodreads.com/book/show/893071.The_Crystal_Bible

Crystal Healing

Unlike the first book, this one is solidly for the laying of the stones as it also tackles about chakras. In fact, it will delve deep only into seven particular stones. The best thing about this book is the fact that it is complete: fully photographed with graphs and charts for better understanding.

http://www.amazon.com/Crystal-Healing-Judy-Hall/dp/18418126
09

Blogs

Crystal Healing For Women

Crystal Healing for Women is also another great resource. Unlike the previous websites that we have mentioned, this blog has a personal touch to it. It explains how crystals can be used at home and how it can help you with common day to day health and emotional problems.

http://www.crystalhealingforwomen.com/blog.html

Hibiscus Moon Crystal Academy

Hibiscus Moon is also a blog styled site, but the difference is, they offer crystal healing courses. There are also many useful articles that can be obtained from their blog like "What it means when your crystal breaks?" and "Dealing With Negative People"

http://hibiscusmooncrystalacademy.com/

Conclusion

Thank you again for downloading this book!

In our lives, we will be faced with many problems: health problems, personal dilemmas, family issues, and stresses at work. All of them are hard to deal with, but we should always take our health as a priority. Why? It's simple, once a health problem surfaces, you'll have to bear the consequences at home, in school, or at work.

At times we will have no choice: we have to resort to medications and hospital confinements, especially if the problem already needs immediate solution. But if it doesn't you won't lose anything from trying the crystal healing method. Actually, if you incorporate the method in your life, you will prevent other diseases from pestering you because crystal healing can strengthen you and it can prevent other health problems from getting worse.

Many people who experienced being healed through the laying of the stones relate that they felt instant relief, but it's still a case to case basis so do not feel frustrated if at the first trials, you felt nothing. May be you are still at the orientation stage.

On a final note, don't rush on choosing the crystals because they will be your companions. Also don't make haste on assessing your own situation-- remember to clear your mind and meditate.

Thank you and good luck!

Printed in Great Britain
by Amazon.co.uk, Ltd.,
Marston Gate.